MW01231048

Avenoir

Poetry & Prose

By

Trisha Leigh Shufelt

Copyright

© Text by Trisha Leigh Shufelt-All Rights Reserved

Cover Art-Baxia Art-Used with Permission

Internal Vector Art-Lisla-Standard License

Moth, Moth, and Raven Art-Trisha Leigh Shufelt

Copy Editor-Candice Louisa Daquin

ISBN- 979-8-218-45545-3

First Printing- June 2024

Imprint Trisha Leigh Shufelt Art In Soul

Massachusetts, USA

Any similarity to real person, living or dead, is coincidental and not intended by the author.

All rights reserved. No part of this book or images may be reproduced or utilized in any means, electronic, or mechanical, including photocopying, recording, or by any information storage and retrieval system, without the prior written permission from the author/publisher except for reviewers who quote brief passages in their review.

Avenoir

POETRY & PROSE

BY

TRISHA LEIGH SHUFELT

ART IN SOUL

*I could tell you my adventures-beginning from this morning,"
said Alice a little timidly; "but it's no use going back to
yesterday, because I was a different person then."*

Alice in Wonderland
Lewis Carroll

To the little girl I forgot to love.

CONTENTS

Avenoir

The desire for memory to flow backwards

The Dictionary of Obscure Sorrows
By John Koenig

Ink

A poet pens words
from marrow's well; inked lines
bleed rivers into seas.

A Haiku

Silent Blackbirds

Let me be more than a moment
more than ink on the brink of breakthrough
more than a decorative ornament
tucked away with no perceived value

let my words stick thick like manuka honey
lace liminal lines beyond space and time
resurrect butterflies from the grave
bleed life into ancient rhymes

let me be a thousand thistle thorns
pricking your skin with unfortunate truths
blossoming balms of forgiveness
mend your scars at their starless roots

let me freeze moments into memory frames
capture cadence steeped in sorrow
wither wraiths whose angel faces
feast on lamenting marrow

let me seal your ghosts behind bell jars
silence their ravenous wants
gather grief fogging its crystalline surface
from mouths whose resonance haunts

let me name the rebellious shadows
who reave peace from your thoughts and then
free them as silent blackbirds
caged forever by the retreating winds.

Seamstress

My brain tires of filling silences—
pervading thoughts,
now moot points,
begun as an empty nest
inside compliant womb—
bleeds waste to my fallow soil

There is no estuary
connecting the dots
only a tongue parched
of its sophistry

Even the breathing air
feels velvet thick
dusk heavy with sigh,
curtaining its eye to
day's discretions

It needles me no more
a ripper strips my seams—
an episiotomy appeasing
the birth of an aborted orphan.

Collecting Shells

Bring me to the shore
of my iniquities,
where I may collect shells
cradle my impurities
and wash dissolute thoughts
in the sounding sea.

I'll take a token,
one broken and unbroken—
a reminder that perfection
is not without abjection,
nor grains
of gritty hidden sand.

A Vignette

frames outside world
it's been here longer than me
it will be here after I am gone
yet this moment of past
tripping over present,
blending future to present again,
I am listening—
bird's song
competing with cascading cars

In between, I am
harkening back to childhood—
longing for a puzzle piece
I cannot hold in my hand
or frame on empty walls

Still, I feel it—
Summer's sigh
breathes over my skin,
and asks, *what seeks you?*

The Art of Overthinking

I'm an artist
a painter, a poet du jour
master of many mediums
with inspiration galore

my art carries a hefty price tag
I'm known by my name
love me or hate me
my art is never the same

you see, the best art is the art
I create in my head at night,
when the world is asleep
art haunts me like the dead

running circles like a roundabout
up and down it goes
a never-ending cycle
of worries and woes,

should haves, what ifs,
and all the layers in between
I keep painting and rewriting,
reworking the unseen

my art is the art of overthinking
but my art masters me
someday, I'll be famous
someday, I'll be free

until that day arrives
my thoughts are my art
ruminating my internal walls
canvasing and framing my heart.

Confessions

Threadbare sentiments
inked from a pensive pen
slip past sleeping stars
washed in watercolors
wounded with want—
uninvited guests
subjugating my thoughts

I ache for safe spaces
between poetry lines
where ink does not barter
to bear pursuing truths
where curated collections
feed confessions
the heart hungers to hear

still, shadows silent
postulating imposters
penetrate with paper tongues
force me inside my disenchanted chest
mock the ever-present echoes
sup on sacred scars
and lick eloquent lines
with lusty countenance

I lay copious sins before deaf priests
who break branches bleeding no blooms
until the nocturn of each snap
yields a symphony of rebellious thorns.

Ministry

The altar of night
is a hymn, dark,
full of possibility
passages I've yet to dream
movie reels spun from
the eye of Creation
all within me echoes
Divine spark
separated by sinew—
a cat's cradle of ambiguity
fashioned by myth and man
the space between
is salt curing the soul
a ministry of starlight
ebbing and flowing
until the burgeoning dawn.

The Quickening

A crow's caw
penetrates a poet's pen
perched above virgin parchment
she ponders a plunge

vacillates between
subject and substance,
grave and sky,
and with a sigh,
the quickening begins
she spirals and scratches

verses nearer to vanish
pain ponders purpose
metaphors mediate
and counter the maelstrom
courting her canal
she cries in rapturous release

now quenched in ink
she clutches her creation
suckling at her quivering breast.

House of Venomous Things

The door is always open
house of venomous things
truth is never spoken
where abject voices sting

discourses to rejection
doubts whispered ear
longings for perfection
mirrors reflecting fears

sabotaging serpents
manipulating history
noxious sorbents
imprinting misery

rewrite
reject
refuse
release.

Your Poetry

Remembrance, let me hear
the quiet parts of you
whisper your retreating dreams

May the petals of percipience,
I failed to perceive
fall from their stubborn shoots
come back and haunt me
as bloodletting thorns

I am ready to bleed your truths
from my ears and drink them
back in like wine

I am eager to open my wounds
release pretenses to the ground
listen as my footprints
sink into reasoning sand
that once trapped me
in hourglass of the past—

I will judge you not
nor will I beg any recompense
for the soil you leave behind

Loss, let me see
the unfiltered parts of you
lift your gossamer sleeve
like the early dawn—
pale, pink, and unencumbered
by teeming day

I see you now
the gift I could not receive
growing beyond the grave
that which I mourned in darkness

I release to the light
for within our crossing paths
gratitude grows
beyond these broken bones

Love, bring me comfort
shawl my shoulders with shadows
for love stretches beyond its gloaming
like resonating stars
guiding me home

Let me feel you lighten the ladened path
with soft moss neith my tender feet
kiss my lips with morning dew
bend my flesh into words

Let me be your poetry
and I will love you
beyond the eternity of time.

Packaging

The wind whispers—
do not seek pain to feel
these are the burdens of time

we fear Doubt's disappointment
thus, we dare not dream
we accept scant offerings, unaware
the contents
we bore from thought
the package
we wrapped from fear

we reave, pit, and prune
pieces of what may be
taper and bend ourselves
into pleasing perceptions
the pallet can accept

truth is a bird
pecking an egg
inside, our boiled thoughts—
dark matter
screaming for the light.

The Silent Wick

Behind the blown candle
smoke mingles
disintegrated thoughts
bind metaphors
wax drippings
ignite epiphanies

silent wick
weave what is
weak within me
onto parched paper
peel poetry from
the marrow of my soul.

The Clock

On a capricious night
life lacks background music
I count the clock—
a metronome
tock-ticks instead of tick-tocks
reduplication runs amuck
a curious linguistic trick
my brain should flip-flop
like King-Kong or
hickory-dickory dock
but each tock
louder than the last tick
flicks an incessant ideation
like a magic trick
ignites a candle wick
and coaxes quick trip
inside surrealistic canvas
across dark corridors
covered in milk box faces
cloaked in smoke
my clumsy fingers
caress cracked glass cloches
reflecting
green shag carpets
leading to
locked coffers lacking keys
where Christmas cards
foxing with age
cushion packed collectibles

curious
I rush past rusty rooms
of restless sleep
where thoughts seep
in over-steeped tea
that sours by the hour
I rise and surmise
attempts to still
this endless ride
as pointless
as a dog chasing its tail
as relentless as
the wind whistling outside
as limitless as
trees whose shadows stretch
like the hands of the living clock
a soundtrack strangling my senses
no longer a slow and steady tock,
but a ceaseless ticking *vivace*.

Tainted

Behind lips sewn shut,
my languid lungs
turn to dust.

Without ablution
thoughts cake
the filter of my voice
till silence is a sin—
tainted nourishment for
this bitter remorse.

I'm Sorry Mother

Mother nature
we are not okay
spill the tea with me
let's open our mouths
take a look inside
our damp, weeping walls
where liquids sour womb
like bitter grapes on withered vine

From what I've heard
we did this to ourselves
cursed you for our chaos
muddied the majestic
too blind to see
your colors do not clash in nature

while it is our colors
contrasting against you
against ourselves
us failing to find you
where you have always been
neith our tissue
leafing our veins
spiraling our skin
nebula and starlight
in our eyes

you said, *I am*
and we did not listen
to our dying breaths.

A World Away

Between the devil and the deep blue sea
eyes do not see
October's drear needle spun sky
weep bloodberry tears

beneath restless cities
black dahlia plumes
mushroom over crumbling clapboard
flesh mixes with rubble

matter merges with molten metal
blanched bones bake
cremation ash
wails with the wind

coats cosmetic indifference
on faraway faces—
those who fail to feel
the weight of distant war.

The Little Girl I Forgot to Love

If you ask me who I was,
I will not be at a loss for adjectives.
The little girl I forgot to love,
still carries words
like fearful, naive, and uncertain
in her pockets.

If you ask me who I am,
I will say I do not know
But the little girl I forgot to love
learned that *no* is a full-stop
whether in deed or words,
one cannot bargain trust,
uncertainty is magical, and
fear often equals regret.

If you ask me who I am becoming,
I will say; stay awhile.
I will show you my pockets,
and you will see they are empty
of weighted words.
They're now filled with love
for the little girl I forgot.

The Good House

There are two sides to every story
and the truth is in the middle; they say...
but what is truth, and what is a lie?

There are facts, but facts
are often accompanied by opinion
and opinion is laced with bias—
who can say with absolute certainty
imprints didn't form their narrative

Then there are stories
you wish you never heard
ones inked with your blood
ones that became crabbed or contrary
ones you ran hither and thither
between your ears
forming an ugly, worn-out carpet

Those, you replayed in glorious technicolor
when the truth was a black and white tale
you shelved for the fable you enabled

Those are the stories
of wasted time and energy
the ones you misunderstood and maligned
the ones you judged by the cover
a tear you cannot mend with a simple stitch

Smote the incessant banter
parading your thoughts—
the lies you formed about yourself
the ones living and breeding
in the good house of your mind.

Arrival

Quick, quick,
the clock strikes a nocturne note
scuttle coal upon the flickering flame,
kettle tea and cast a magick mote

storms shake the sleepy trees—
the day darkens to dreary dusk,
cleaves the leaves, and slakes the earth
with sodden, sticky rust

chill coats the cracked windowsill
brusk, black rook, leases a broken limb,
cocks his crooked beak, and croaks
into the wicked winter wind,

"Autumn is no more."

Butterfly Effect

Nemesis eyes him
in the rearview mirror
watching him
inject a mad river
into his sacred veins—
butterfly effect of past choices
catches up—
a long-ago inescapable demon
wears uneasily like the *Shirt of Nessus,*
cooks him alive with black snow
falling from November's unforgiving sky
into rock bottom's shallow grave
where death is closer than it appears.

Castaways

Something new
is something old
surfaces my thoughts
like a breaching whale
spews forth briny bits
of backscatter bullshit
castaways
from an abandoned island
rerun too many times

there is no rescue ship
this vessel is fish food
for the fathomless.

Blue Shadows

In the hushing silence before sleep,
where the day-dying embers fade
to an open door,
step through, lucid and lithe

Fall into the blue shadows, deep with sigh
remember, all that you have forgotten
resonates in that undertow

There, in the darkness of dreams,
your soul is speaking.

The Butcher

She knelt before the butcher
her sins he'd shrive—the priest
his perched form above her
shrike eyes masked deceit

She cupped his sacrament—
eager flesh inside hopeful hands
as talons tangled her nest of hair,
slaughtered offerings
from another lamb

She swallowed his holy juice,
acidulous in its serpent ease
as the sibilance of his sigh
seeped and drowned
her sodden silent pleas

No absolution found her
only trust and innocence, lost—
her prayers, she left before him
impaled upon his cross.

Autumn's Funeral

Tree-strewn berries
burst open blood jewel eyes
bleed, *I am*
from veiny leaves mantling
the unforgiving gravel ground
largesse neith Autumn's fragile flesh
a repast for ravenous blackbird's mouth.

Sick

You had me trapped—
me, a sick little bird
caged inside sanitary walls
your fingers at my throat
in mock examination, while
what was limp between us
pressed with urgency
against my pre-teen knees

Did it harden your resolve
when I cast my eyes downward
or make me a better victim
when a compressed tongue
silenced every compulsion
I had to scream?

Dr. D, you overshadowed me
and made damn sure
your nurse couldn't see my eyes
as you leaned in with a lick
of your chapped lips—
breath hot and vile
with manipulation
as though to say,
I am an adult, and you
will not be seen, nor heard.

The Art Collectors

Creatures of insatiable hunger
kneel before tempting teats
weighted in malignant milk

submissive, they suckle servitude
bellies bloated, content to comply
or bury their eyes into bias's breasts

madness mounting by minutes
declension's downward spiral
rendering ever with Machiavellian hands
anything they want, yet everything they want
feeds futility of no intrinsic value—

Apathetic art on a corrupt canvas,
created with a parasitic paintbrush
that swims in a sea of ruddled paint,
results in a collective simulacrum
only the egoist can appreciate.

The Blackening Brae

Tethered, they trust tainted fields
mindlessly moving about their day
despite analogous threads they yield
despite outliers watching the brae.

It's bias that binds their fragile fate
grows fat upon their sleeping wool
whose grazed gorse perceptions make
in echo chambers presumptuous whorl.

Blithely, they bleat and swan the blackening brae
weave weighted wings from predictive pores
until fallacy shakes opaque eyes awake—
the inevitable slaughtering storms.

Painter

Your essence bleeds in my darkness
life-giving, purposeful
rain to the soil, earth to birth

your touch, layers of texture
edged with ambient twilight
echoes chaos and love

in each stroke
a fine line
precise and poignant

art in the flesh
water and oil
pigments from past seasons
framed inside gold

I have come to realize
you painted me
or I, you, long ago
before we were born
before thought became reality
there was an idea of us

alive with allegory
a story returning from memory
a seed planted in shadow
like whispered fables
remembered in our veins
vining beneath our skin.

Ghost Apples

Everything I write
clutches the stem
clings to the vine
never ripening
eats me from the inside out—
a worm I cannot conquer

Am I fated to sleep
behind rime ice and glass,
to dream of becoming—
bright blossom
favored by the sun
a feast for your eyes
to pluck and press me
between pages of poetry

Please,
have this fruit
share the dark with me, feast—
the insides of this ghost apple
are *not* for everyone to see.

Cork

This is the truth
I refused to see
the trapped cork
bobbing in the sea
was *me*
and this me, drank
the sanguine sea
swelled in its blood
let it tinge my skin rosy red
let it grieve my lungs to breathe
beyond scent of sorrow
beyond gluttonous grip
of Inebriation's purple prose
I tripped willingly
into Anxiety's bed and fell
let the lies I disencumbered
swell
and swell
and swell.

This was the truth
I refused to see
the red sea had swallowed me—
inside a green glass horizon,
I labeled my vacant shell
outside, I colored it
to hide my copious hell.

Attic

My thoughts rent an attic space
desperate to shine
where memories mingle with dust motes,
and every creak is an awaiting rhyme

I long to put pen to paper
write poetry on its peeling walls
hang tapestries and timepieces
fill the shelves with books and dolls

there are times when it leaks lost secrets
times, when matches struck, won't burn
times when the windows are nailed shut,
and times I long to never return

but this attic is of my own making
a space I rent from me
whatever I've lost, I've found within it,
and the ghosts haunt it for free.

Storms

This time
I will enjoy thunder
bask in downpours
filing dark spaces
within me
fear not depth
nor drowning

I will become
its energy until
veins vining
neith my skin
ignite lightning rods
limbs rise like a mighty oak
blood boils my sodden soil

This time, I will scream
my light across the sky.

Wednesday's Child is Full of Woe

tired of listening to
the voices in her head
rewinding battles
resurrecting the dead
typing words, she'll backspace
into invisibility
being a trapped bird
in hourglass sands of infinity
fear when she's walking
anywhere alone
uncertainty when she strays
too far from home
loneliness of entering empty rooms
ghosts that lean too closely
from open wounds
covering the pain with
a masked or brave face
the past that lingers in scars
she can't erase
lip-bitten truths
she covers with her hands
screams that well inside
no one understands
dreams that drown her
in slack brown water
time she can no longer
beg, steal, or barter
Somewhere in life,
Wednesday lost her sense of self

49

filed her dreams away with
the books on her shelf
tonight, she will drift away
into unconsciousness
where her pain slips the stream
into nothingness.

Dark Mother

The woman I see
stares back at me
she does not lie
she knows me
better than I know myself

she shows me who I am
behind fine lines
dispels spells cast
with potions and powders

she eyes my surroundings
fortunate and fake
comforts for
the disquieting wake
and smiles

each morning
despite the presentation
she sees the mask
beyond the surface
she sees layers ripple
she sees the child beneath
drown and disappear

in her place
a dark mother rises
floats to the mirror-lake surface
and stares at me like a dead fish.

(Inspired by Sylvia Plath's Mirror)

The Ties that Bind

October made me sober
slapped sleep from my eyes
what worked yesterday is over
no more masks to disguise

I've lost my will to wonder
between yesterday and the next
excuses no longer hinder
chaos chomping at the bliss

I know my ancestors are watching
my demons pour down the drain
and with them, any pausing
I might reconsider or refrain

The choice is pretty simple
control it, or let it control me
trade deception for conception
inebriation for sobriety.

Swing Coat

Lady Lazarus, I tried you on for size
slipped your skin's bright lampshade over mine
found myself in a swing coat of black onyx
curious treasures in deep, woolen pockets

My fingers sank into the mysterious abyss
scrapped barnacle walls of metaphors and madness
raked razor-edge pencils, teeth-bitten and worn
cut apprehensions on mirror shards and storms

Emersed, I swam with your disquieting muses
channel crossing the dead dears, lost in confusion
I floated among the *peanut-crunching crowd*,
despite apprehensions, I dove as deep as fear allowed

Surfaced above the dark wood, dark water
sat near Polly's tree with the beekeeper's daughter
saw a rook playing Ouija with a shrike and an owl
sang a strumpet song with a spider and a sow

I traipsed through a November graveyard
coupled with dust in the shadow of a stone
ate mushrooms in the manor garden
until moonrise and full fathom five called me home.

Italicized lines from Sylvia Plath's Lady Lazarus 1962
and Witch Burning 1959

53

Terms

I accepted the anger my questions received.
I denied the peace restored by my truth.
I added the pleasure your answers gave.
I subtracted the pain destroyed by your lies.

In the end,
I found the sum
didn't justify the means.

Tattoos

We bloomed bruises to heal
what petaled poetry could not,
tattooed sigils on our skin
with sharp-tongued needles
and licked our ragged edges
with the precision of a lathe.

Beneath borrowed time
we bore the brunt of bedlam
we begged to breed.

The Unsaid

The *unsaid* bleeds
poison seeps pernicious perfume
smacks the air with a baleful glare
unsung verses loop and bloom

The *unsaid* sheds
under the bed where retention rusts
layers remain without ablution, stains
stir the animus and rouse the dust

The *unsaid* feeds
silent shadows reaved and saved
eternity stews its marinated brew
ravened marrow by the hungry grave.

Hive Mind

No middle ground
in between
numb
a slow, steady beat
a rhythmic drum
in between
thoughts
dumb
bees hum
hive mind
a home
inside
words swim
salt and sour
a vine climbing
a crumbling tower
nothing satiates
what it devours
in between
a breath and a death.

The Restless Room

An unhinged door opens
a thousand ghosts hang
like dust sheets
sepia memories sag
with weighted words
concatenated by pointillist dots
inside matted frames

affixed to walls
they tighten and fold
like yellow petals
retreating into buds
hide as pareidolia
neith sallow stained paper
till scored and stripped
she emerges

bleeding deadheaded corpuscles
to the floor
where pretense's peeled layers
reveal her truth—
no longer worn deep,
her metaphors retreat
into reality's restless room.

Inspired by The Yellow Wallpaper by Charlotte Perkins Gilman 1892

Lady Mag

where have you been—
out hiding shiny objects
or unearthing them again

I miss your black-and-white pies
bejeweled in raiment finery
I miss your surprises in disguise
and the winterberries
you left for me

Gone are your roving suiters
fruit laced with succulent sorrow
boys perched pretty
on my windowsill
songs of joy
and lost tomorrows

They took the girl
I used to know
replaced her wishes with a kiss—
Devil's blood
hidden under her tongue
skullduggery from the abyss

They traded her words
of silver and gold
now, shrills and trills
of chattery banter
buried her voice neith

deep, dank earth
along with her secrets
and her laughter

For health and wealth,
owned by the Devil himself
until skiving her blood-tongue-free
no rhymes, no words,
only nonsense is heard
in the voices squawking
back at me.

Adapted from the Magpie Nursery Rhyme.

Moths

Your words
light sullen shadows
release sleepy moths
from hidden core
wingtips crackle
flames of cindered paper
assailing woodworm floor

Your words
mend my tattered edges
fold me up
like precious silk
embroidered
metaphors and similes
golden thread on wintered wilt

Your words
raise memories
awaken silent shoots
time forgot
bred from splintered thoughts
sap limning buried bruises
on fruit made sweet from rot

Your words
pinned to paper
moths foxing with time

written balm
encased in tomes
ash to ink,
your words found a home.

Black Moon Lilith

Black moon Lilith sees me
hiding behind antique lace—
a child inside
a crone's shell
vulnerable to the elements
exposed in my hell—

a blown wick from
her mirror mouth
like a celestial whisper
unsheathes my dis ease
she showers me in shadows
washes dirges with ease

the wantonness of a lover
she licks lies from
my darkened well
dives deep into
my withered womb—
discordant dead now dwell

she sups sin
from my stories
without malice,
yet lacking sympathy
picks my bones clean
of melancholy's marrow
devours secrets sewn
from malignancy

she leaves me,
a quivering moth
beating bedlam from
my broken wings
Black Moon Lilith
reaves me
silent amidst
her blackbird sting.

Spinner's Loom

A Spinner weaves neath the moon
drop spindle pirouettes in her hand
fleeces sway on branches broon
spider webs of fugacious strands

drafting down the magical lume
roving reeling on mystic loom
feathering fibers escape the skein
into wind, motes float and spoom

our choices, she cannot augur
no thread can she shift or shape
in mortal matters, she mustn't barter
Free Will's conception wake

through season, time, and heaven above
she spins our threads til old and frayed—
how when we die our shades will rove
when she has hushed our woven ways.

Adapted from the Indian to his Love by William Butler Yeats-1886

Queen of Swords

I am the Queen of Swords
spinning thoughts into ink
merging marrow into steel
madness and mindfulness
in balanced proportions bleed
from my sword-shaped tongue

I am the mourning October
silver sinew, moonstruck
a woeful waif upon world
weighted with
shadow-swept sorrow

I am the cawing corvid's cry
cloaked in fury's ashen storm
supping upon inequity's face
I fall, and rise like Lazarus
I am wise with winged wrath—

An alchemical chaos
equipoised to slice serpent throats
or blossom bellicose blades from
the mouths of the meek.

Beloved

You say
I never write about you
yet, you are
the breath of me

You are beneath
my surface—
a collision to my senses
in every penned line—

You are
the dark and
the light of me,
merging from
a book of shadows
I feared to open

You are
a conduit for my ink
a mirror, uncovering
the asperity of my edges,
the chaos in scars—
the beauty in me,
I refused to see

You are
the words once caged
but now free—
letters to my past,
mailed to my future self
quills in my wings

who I was
who I am
who I'm yet to be

You are
a spoken vow

You are
the ones unsaid
the first time
you looked at me.

The Singeless Moth

You appear as a moth
out of the oven, un-singed
light in your wings
never needing to lean
toward the moon

you are luminescent
a lit candle
heat igniting
my thoughts of you.

Scars

I wonder if scars asseverate
lessons of lifetimes past—
surface as war wounds
weaved from within—
life writing poetry
on our skin

death is not a full stop
the rhymes roundabout
history's mystery of mysteries
we must master
what defaces our tome
to efface our parchment pristine.

Overheard on a Walk

Who seized my leaves,
cried the barren trees

No one
sighed the breeze
alas, you fail to remember
it comes every September
Summer's dying embers
stir you to surrender
colors before Winter fleeces
the ground with white

The trees shook
with a click and a clack
shivered
with a creak and a crack
will my painted leaves come back

Not those,
blew the breeze
they belong to
the burrows and the bees
to the bugs beneath
the rotting fruit
resolute to dream
silent in their sleeping mute

Will I forget them,
beseeched the trees

Never
eased the breeze
I will stir them
neith you like memories
we'll delight as they dance
and reminisce as they pass
I'll roll them over
your hidden roots
until new leaves awaken
with Spring's green shoots.

Arranging Flowers

Your words are a witch burr
piercing tendered trust—
sharp and painful
reverberating in minor key
deep in my bones
warning cells
take notice
fight or flee—

bitter sobriety
coats bitten lips, strips
sandpaper tongue
of its sting
a quick lick
I cannot stick

Retreat then
into smoky rooms
clouded in doubt
my response
no more than
a cacophony of cicadas
incoherent in their song

you smile
arrange me like flowers
snip off pieces
discard the wilt
drown the rest

until I'm pretty and perfect
inside a fragile vase
you display with pride.

I am

I am in my books. I am the secret between **the**
lines. I am the innuendo in a **song.**
I am frayed, dog-eared, and dusty. I am torn **from**
time, pencil marked, stained, and spine worn. I am **the**
echo of a thousand poet's cries lifted from the **cathedral**
of their minds, spilling into sentient rhymes **of**
measured meter. I am him and **her,**
my father, mother, and the **mouth**
of every sister and brother who **would**
wear their weight freely and **fall**
head first into darkened sediment, if only **to**
awaken a few by their shadowed sentiments. I am **the**
the broken body on the **floor**-
a crow-picked carrion, festering **like**
a confession on **a**
whore, whose lips have been sewn shut by a **lie.**

*A golden shovel poem inspired by
Frieda Hughes' poem, Medusa.*

Bookmarks

I spin you
on the edge of a poem
make love to words
I've yet to write
face the reality
of faded whispers
as thoughts dry ink
in unreceptive pen

It is there
I'll keep you
fold images in my mind
until the flush of Autumn
awakens your pages
in colors fit to rhyme.

Found

Humming cicadas
dragged dense wind
and with it, Summer's breath
exhaled rancid Hawthorn

I found you,
surceased of sanctuary,
not in a bower bed
but reposed in reeds

I found you,
purloined of pelt—
your petal pale flesh, slime-slick,
stuck with milkweed seeds,
and wriggling pearl clusters

I found you,
a tattooed snapshot,
bunny burrowed
in the back of my brain

Wet blind,
I sheaved clover,
placed sprigs near your nose,
and prayed

Our button-brown eyes
begged heavenward,
but our mouths muted—
sewn shut by dragonflies

Our prayers met deaf ears—
once again discarded
among the deadhead daisies
and trailer park trash.

Black Dog

I'm heading to the river
it's a place I often dwell
black dog as my companion
blacker than fathomless well

I did not ask for him
he found me, you might say
a door to a distant memory
I'm still opening today

He never leaves or wanders
though we both are often lost
there are times I wish he'd leave me
and our paths had never crossed

I've yet to name him
too many names come to mind
moreover, I've yet to tame him
despite my efforts this time

And so, we head to the river
black dog by my side
shedding shadows deciphered
bearing others, we deem to hide.

Frozen

Sudden wind shocks
the mourneress

Vitreous parlays shatter
behind parted lips,
copper impurities cascade
and flow into lakes
where fire-fleeing horses
plunge and freeze fables
in their warring wake.

Inspired by Curzio Malaparte book Kaputt,
in which he describes fire-fleeing horses that become trapped
in a lake that flash freezes from a sudden wind.

An Unquiet Mind

An unquiet mind
stores fears in Mason jars
creates labels for a pantry of pain
bakes scattered thoughts in broken ovens
til insanity starts to feel sane

An unquiet mind
never sleeps where density drowns
neith her cave of weighted covers
shadows stalk and demons deceive
thoughts that hibernate as lovers

An unquiet mind
motes the air with latent memories
and pecks the soul to bleed
unsaid filaments that vein the walls
from grief's tangled, goring weed

An unquiet mind
ignites restless rooms with fallacious fire
blazes her fevered, fervent wick
never satiates what burns beneath
walls that blacken quick, quick, quick.

Falling

I'm a bird hitting a window
blindsided by a sign
falling without wings
my fluted bones brace
for gravel ground
bee stings

Rain muddies my landing
childish tears swallowed
in confusion, lost to trust
bruises blossom bright cerise
before ripe blackening plums
leave me Reality's rust.

Wintering

Lips purse probing wood
premature Winter womb
a dusty moth quivers
tissue paper thin
as eves grieve
collapse, curl, and
retreat in fetal defeat

How naive
when weighted globes, cleaved
her pleasures, thieves seized
what was left
in her reckoning wake

She was an orchard
hot, ripe, sweet, and esculent
et without regret
fresh fruit, her seasons bore
before blood drained
now barren core—
no longer a sinful succulent

Thief!
you left her no quarter
left her nothing to barter
left her as a shriveled, arid vine
swelling no further
you left her only with time.

A Day

A burn hole stops the moment
forces my mouth shut
clamps a barrette
thoughts flake like dead skin
still, I stand in sober silence
thrown back into childhood
small and insignificant
as letters, numbers,
and my son's laughter
fade into distant memory

chaos consumes the canvas
I call my mother
confused, craving comfort
concerns come
followed by another plane
slicing steel with ease—
a knife through a birthday cake

We are under attack
your words bomb my ears
I swallow; the reality
explodes in my stomach.

Cruel Thorns

The black glass sky envelops **everything**
except me, as though **I**
am bitter to taste and foul to **touch**.
Even the moon **with**
her ever-watchful eye offers no **tenderness**
and turns away in her celestial crescent. **Alas,**
the stars share no sympathy either. Pestilence **pricks**
at my heart and weeps my bruised skin **like**
fruit caught in the cruel thorns of **a**
bushes **bramble**.

Haiku by Kobayashi Issa

Breathless

You are *born of the very sigh that silence heaves*
when Winter sleeves the world with white
you are a prayer on the tongue of hope
longing for an answer

you are a kaleidoscope of color
as changing as the sea
as present as the tides
that teems my thoughts
yet sobers these penned lines

I dare not dance too closely
or summon your shadows
to do so would deplete me
like my breath you steal
upon entering the room.

Italicized line-I Stood Tip-Toe Upon a Little Hill by John Keats

The View

A broken window
fractures view
exposes vulnerable facade
framed in wooden box

Do truths escape
splintered spectrum,
or do colors
igniting glass to dance
remind us of what used to be
before fingers gripped
throwing stones?

Truce

Back to the Land of Silver and Spoons
where cracked teacups never leak
bird and beast lay side by side
and neither dare to seek
retribution despite venomous air
picking their teeth clean of ire
drinking machinations, ilk, and woe
tending temper's tenacious fire

poets in the damning dark
raising pens instead of swords
choosing ink over spilling blood
healing memory's copious wars.

Green Bicycle

Forget me not
cried the little girl
hiding in the hedgerow,
choking on her tears,
and the falling rain

No longer latched to a key,
she's all grown up now
taking deep drinks
of cloying mantras
and passionless prose—
pretty words
poured from a paper cup

Till she retches
on poisoned lines lacking pith
toxic positivity that fails to satiate
what needs healing
what needs screaming—
brontide, she's been brewing for years
braids her skin like bark
and rings her insides with sickness

she should shore to the core
and let the ground grieve
her losses into peat.

Ride or Die

Do you see her soul
unfurled wings
open like a book
inviting you inside
to ride or die

Do you see her mind
scarab beetle roiling
in metallic mist
blackening ember
neith a swollen sky
a deep pine forest
a dusky hue of sigh

Do you see her
as she truly is
wildflower blossom
conforming for no one
a tempest among the trees
an echo in the wind
a swirl of Autumn leaves

She is all these and more
Queen of her Eden
bending boughs
of ripened truths—
downfall for hungry mouths
craving only orchard fruits.

Ancestral Gardens

And she said,
you will feel all that came before you—
all their strife and stolen solace
will slice you open,
core the rot from your fruit

you will hit the ground
plumbed of spirit
bruised and broken

you will crumble into stones
each one an ancestor's name
you cannot remember but
feel nonetheless, heavy
on the tip of your tongue

you will swallow them as bitter pills
feel their weight and woe
anchor you to the earth
as the memory of their mistakes
mock every incessant excuse
that rages and twists your insides
into knots, begging to be unraveled—

mysteries of why they failed
and you are here, burdened
with their battlements,
teeth, bones, and blood

you will break their chains
you will set them free
and they will gape
in awe and gratitude
for your strength.

Another Poet

Am I another poet
destined to die,
fingers full of pills,
poisoned on poetry pie

spiral descent
into madness' well
my baked words
fresh from oven hell

raven shaped dough
bite my battered core
drink my ink—my overthink
Would you care for more?

scatter my ashes to the wind
consume the dark
and remember when
words like stars
ignite the sky

in the end
they'll shake their heads
and wonder why.

Avenoir

When I am gone
when all who remember
disappear
when lines of succession
dry and blow away
as forgotten autumn leaves
who will find these words—
say, I know her
I was her
I could have loved her
I see her
I honor her
hold her close to my heart
underline soul whispers
drink in blood and marrow's ink

Will it be me
grown from the grave
swollen blossom
avenoir, beckoning backward
speaking to *my soul*
come to find me
dog-eared with age
and bring me home.

My flames grow with age
brighter neith darkening skies
burning the past down!

AUTHOR THOUGHTS

Mirror, mirror on the wall, poetry resides within us all.

A mirror, or looking glass, is a surface that reflects an object, person, or image due to light bouncing off it. The earliest known mirror was water. Remember the Greek myth of Narcissus, who fell in love with his own reflection. Vanity, wisdom, duality, light, shadow, illusion, deception, or distortion—mirrors have long, fabled histories, rich symbolism, and stories to tell. Whether it be Feng Shui or a selfie, humankind has never fallen out of love with mirrors. Mirrors are thought to reveal the truth and are symbolic conduits for introspection; however, our internal lens may cloud the picture of what we ultimately perceive as truth.

Avenoir. An unusual word that is not likely a part of one's everyday vocabulary. I love unusual words. I came across it after picking up a copy of *The Dictionary of Obscure Sorrows* by John Koenig. According to Koenig, *avenoir* is French for avenir, future plus *avoir*, to have. It means the desire to see your memories flow backward. Koenig's posits that our unknown life moves forward while we, as rowers, have our back to the future. We are facing the past but our memories are behind us. But what if we changed direction? We would face our past, see it unfold, the mistakes, the moments shared, important turning points, problems solved before anticipated. Eventually, life as we know it would become a blank canvas again. It's the ultimate life review. He goes on to say, "The world would finally earn your trust. Nothing left to remember, nothing left to regret, with your whole life laid out in front of you and your whole life left behind."

In many respects, isn't this the heart of poetry? As a poet, I spend much time rowing my boat backward, facing the past, coming to terms with feelings, and sometimes writing letters to my history to heal old wounds. This journeyed collection is an avenoir, a mirror or portal to the past. It's a deep dive to uncover my truth and the universal truth of how going backward is sometimes the key to moving forward. I've gained much from the journey. I hope you will, too.

Trisha Leigh

Acknowledgements

Andy & Patrick-It should go without saying, but you both are the heart of me.

Candice Louisa Daquin- Poet to my Soul. My deepest gratitude to you for your support and friendship.

Christine E. Ray-Thank you for your support of my work.

My readers-I wouldn't be doing this without your love and support. I am truly grateful.

Barbara from Baxia Art for her beautiful cover-I'm so grateful to work with you again.

~~~~~~

About Avenoir text sources-The Dictionary of Obscure Sorrows by John Koenig ©2021 Simon & Schuster

Golden Shovel Poetry Line by Frieda Hughes-Medusa

Inside Dark Pockets- Italicized lines from Sylvia Plath's Lady Lazarus 1962 and Witch Burning 1959, as well as various Plath titles.

Breathless- Italicized line-I Stood Tip-Toe Upon a Little Hill by John Keats 1817

ABOUT THE AUTHOR

Trisha Leigh Shufelt is an award-winning poet, self-taught mixed media artist, and breast cancer survivor. Trisha's work leans toward confessional poetry with an emphasis on nature and gothic imagery. She often draws upon her own experience with addiction, anxiety, and loss. She is the author of several poetry books, including *The Ghosts of Nevermore*, winner of a 2023 Saturday Visiter Award from the Edgar Allan Poe House and Museum in Baltimore, MD. Her work has also appeared in several poetry anthologies.

Poetry Books by the Author

Liminal Lines- Poetry & Prose
Liminal Lessons- Poetry & Prose
Break & Bloom-Poetry & Prose
The Ghosts of Nevermore-Poetry, Prose & Short Stories
inspired by the works of Edgar Allan Poe- *2023 Saturday Visiter Award Winner through the Poe House & Museum of Baltimore, MD.*
The Ghosts of Winterbourne-Poetry & Prose
Sunder the Silence-Poetry & Prose
Unearthing Nevermore-Golden Shovel Poetry Inspired by Edgar Allan Poe

Poetry & Short Story Anthologies, Magazines, and online publications

Evermore-Raven's Quoth Press
300 South Street Publishing-
Love is Helpless
Immortal Tales
Shadow of the Soul
Quail Bell
Heretics, Lovers, and Madmen

Published under the pen Andaleigh Archer include-

The Underwood Wicked Fairytale Series
Underwood-A Wicked Beginning
Thorn Apple-A Wicked Spell
Quietus-A Wicked Ending
Maeve-A Wicked Beginning

The Promise ~A Faerie's Tale

Artist & Author works through Schiffer Publishing/RedFeatherMBS include-

The Poe Tarot- *Nominated for a 2022 Saturday Visiter Award through the Poe House & Museum of Baltimore, MD & winner of a Bronze 2022 COVR Visionary Award.* The Everglow Divination System

Other works include-
Passion for Poetry-A poetry review journal for poets and poetry lovers

You can find out more about Trisha at
www.spilltheteapoetry.com
https://trishaleighshufelt.substack.com
www.artinsoul.org

Made in the USA
Columbia, SC
19 August 2024

f99ebe14-cb53-4c2f-a189-ea9f1caac68fR01